OCEARCH
Sharks in the Ocean

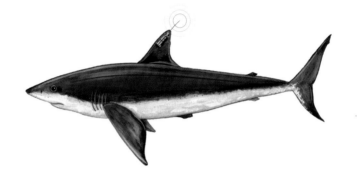

Written by Katharine Baumgartner
Illustrated by Jeffrey C. Domm

Printed in USA

Ocean Family Games, Inc.
Port Charlotte, Florida

info@oceanfamilygames.com
www.oceanfamilygames.com

Dedications
This book is in dedication to OCEARCH for their devotion to accelerate the ocean's return to balance and abundance through shark research and education. This book was written to teach why sharks are important and what actions we can take to protect shark populations and, ultimately, the oceans.
Katharine Baumgartner

Take action today to combat our climate crisis. The oceans and forests can only be restored by your desire to do so. Volunteer, donate, speak up, and pitch in to solve this serious threat to us all.
Jeffrey C. Domm

About the Author:

Katharine Baumgartner grew up in Michigan. Her love for aquatic life and conservation led her to a degree in fisheries and wildlife management from Michigan State University. After college, Katharine moved to the Florida Keys where she taught marine science education and trained marine scientists. Afterwards, Katharine went on to teach science in the Florida public school system before becoming a stay-at-home mother. Today, Katharine and her family live near Venice, Florida, the shark tooth capital of the world. It is here where Katharine combined her love for the ocean, educating others, and playing games to start a business, Ocean Family Games.

About the Illustrator:

Jeff Domm is a wildlife illustrator with more than 30 published kids books and field guides in the USA and Canada. His clients have included the Smithsonian Institution, Bedford Institute of Oceanography, Canada Department of Fisheries and Oceans, and Parks Canada. Jeff has a BFA in design/illustration from the Detroit Centre for Creative Studies and an MA in film from Chicago Columbia. He teaches illustration, drawing, and design at NSCAD University in Halifax. His studio is in a small village along the North Atlantic coast in Cow Bay, Nova Scotia.

Guild of Natural Science illustrators member
www.jeffdommportfolio.com

Ocean
Family Games

Ocean Family Games was founded with a mission to create ocean-themed games and children's books that educate people on the importance of our oceans and how to help protect them. As an ocean-friendly business, Ocean Family Games proudly manufactures products plastic free and a portion of all sales goes toward marine science education and research. Follow us on social media or visit www.oceanfamilygames.com to help us support the ocean and learn what exciting new books and games are next!

Play Games. Save Oceans.

OCEARCH

OCEARCH is a data-centric organization built to help scientists collect previously unattainable data in the ocean. Their mission is to accelerate the ocean's return to balance and abundance, through fearless innovations in scientific research, education, outreach, and policy, using unique collaborations of individuals and organizations in the USA and abroad.
To learn more and track sharks in real time, visit www.ocearch.org.

Spot the seagull
A friendly seagull calls out to you on every page.
See if you can spot all 22 seagulls hidden in each of the pages but
do not include these four.

Sharks are an important part of the ocean,
they balance the sea like a magic potion.

When too many sharks are taken away,
the rest of the animals don't want to stay.

To understand more about sharks and how they grow,
OCEARCH heads out to see where they go.

They work together with scientists on board their ship,
to research sharks and learn more with every trip.

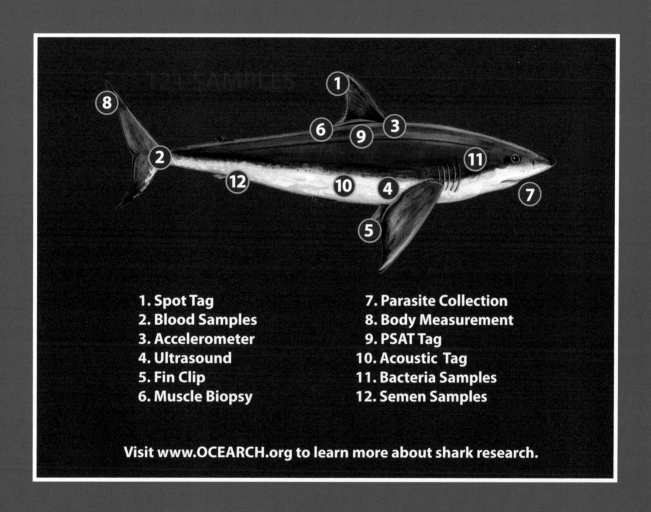

1. Spot Tag
2. Blood Samples
3. Accelerometer
4. Ultrasound
5. Fin Clip
6. Muscle Biopsy

7. Parasite Collection
8. Body Measurement
9. PSAT Tag
10. Acoustic Tag
11. Bacteria Samples
12. Semen Samples

Visit www.OCEARCH.org to learn more about shark research.

OCEARCH has caught and tagged sharks
such as Katharine, Cabot, and Mary Lee.

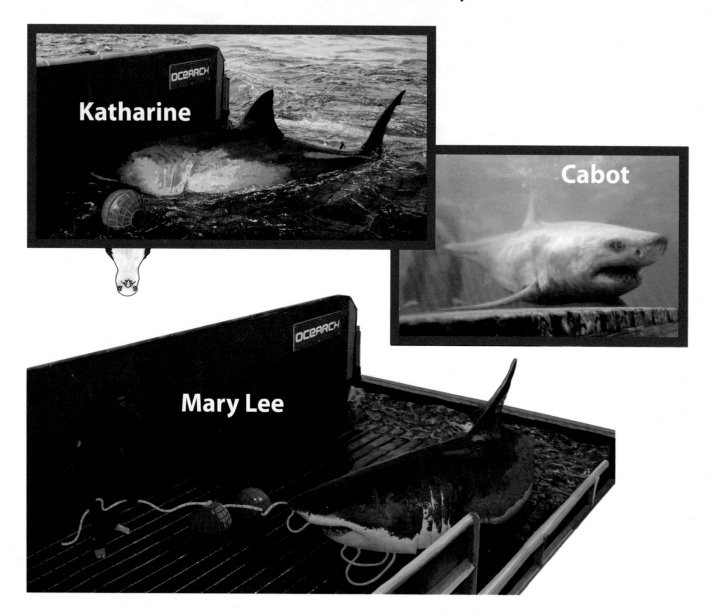

They are studied on a special lift,
for less than 15 minutes and then set free.

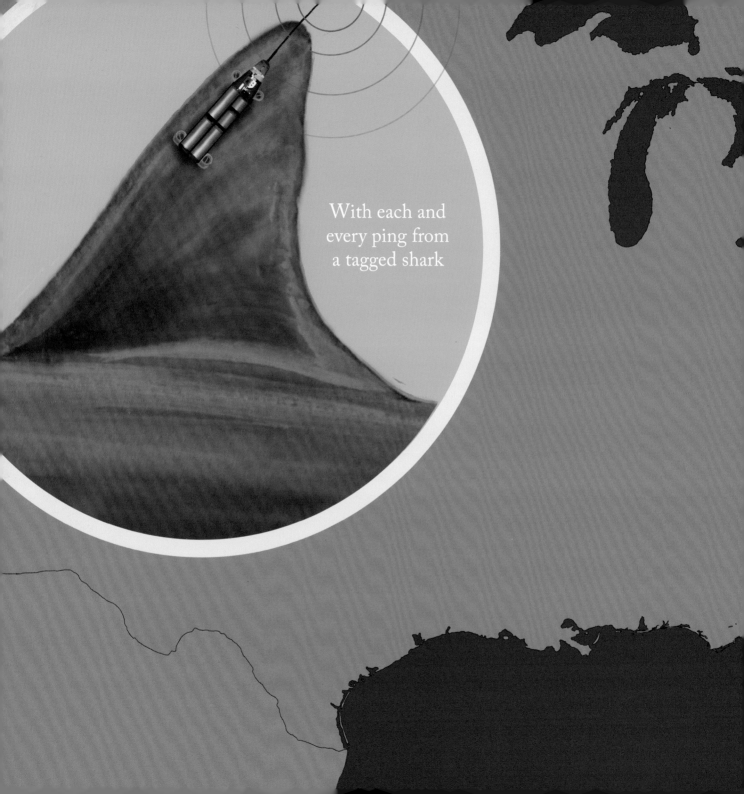

With each and
every ping from
a tagged shark

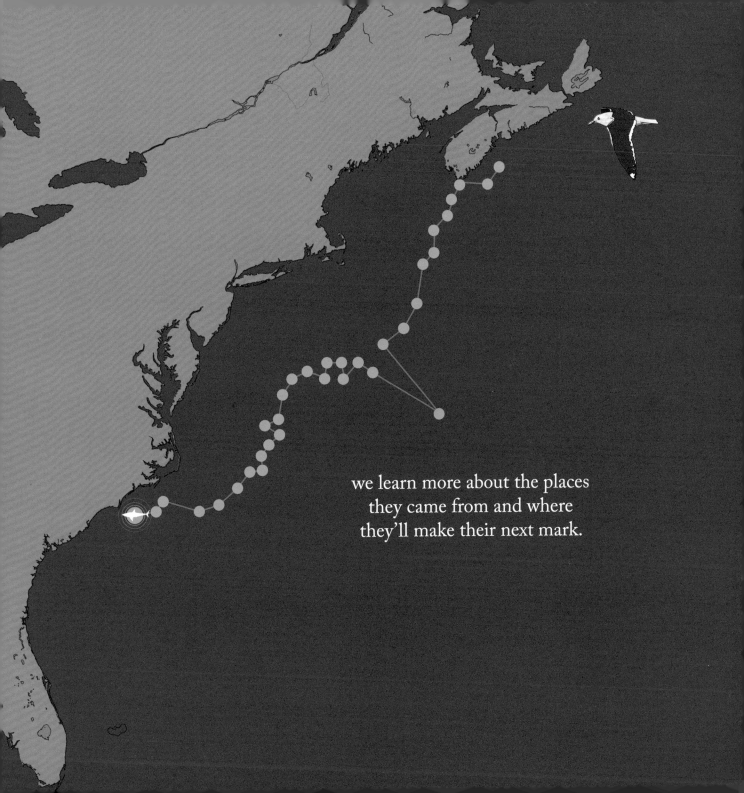

we learn more about the places
they came from and where
they'll make their next mark.

This helps us to solve the white shark puzzle

because now we can see where
grown-up sharks go to snuggle.

By tracking female sharks we learn
where nursery areas are found.

These are places baby sharks are born
so they can grow up safe and sound.

Scientists piece all of this information together
then send it to lawmakers who protect the
sharks and our oceans forever.

With all of this hard work being done...

We still need your help, which can be lots of fun.

You can volunteer your time
with an organization for their sake,

gather with friends to clean up
near a park, beach, or lake.

You can reduce the plastics
that you use in a day.

REDUCE

REUSE

Or eat seafood that has been caught
in an environmentally friendly way.

Sea Turtles and small fish swim free.

It's important for all of this to be done to preserve the oceans for generations to come.